ber's, Naurice.

r   isneros.

HENRY CISNEROS

Henry Cisneros addresses the 1984 Democratic
National Convention in San Francisco.

HENRY CISNEROS
A Leader for the Future

By Naurice Roberts

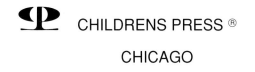 CHILDRENS PRESS ®

CHICAGO

Cover: Henry G. Cisneros

p. 3 From left to right: Helen Ayala, president of C.O.P.S.; Henry Cisneros, mayor of San Antonio; Maria Berrizobal, city council member at a planning meeting for Vista Verde South

p.31 Cisneros is sworn in as a member of Bill Clinton's cabinet on January 12, 1993.

Picture Acknowledgements:

Wide World Photos — 1, 31

Journalism Services/©Oscar Williams — Cover, 2, 3, 6 (left), 14, 15, 17, 18, 19 (2 photos), 20 (3 photos), 22, 23, 24 (2 photos), 25

Courtesy of Central Catholic Marianist High School — 5, 10 (2 photos)

UPI/Bettman Newsphotos — 26, 29

San Antonio Convention & Visitors Bureau — 6 (right), 7, 8 (2 photos)

Texas A & M University — 13 (2 photos)

Project Editor: E. Russell Primm
Design and Electronic Composition: Biner Design

Library of Congress Cataloging-in-Publication Data

Roberts, Naurice.
    Henry Cisneros: a leader for the future / by Naurice Roberts.
    p. cm. — (A picture story biography)
    Summary: A biography of the San Antonio mayor who became the first Mexican-American mayor of a major city.
    ISBN 0-516-04175-4
    1. Cisneros, Henry — Juvenile literature. 2. Mayors — Texas — San Antonio — Biography — Juvenile literature. 3. Mexican Americans — Texas — San Antonio – Biography — Juvenile literature. 4. San Antonio (Tex.) — Biography — Juvenile literature. [1. Cisneros, Henry. 2. Mayors. 3. Mexican Americans] I. Title. II. Series: Picture-story biographies.

F394.S2C5667 1991   91-2330
976.4'351063'092—dc20   CIP
[B]   AC

1964 class picture

Who is Henry G. Cisneros, and why is he important?

Henry Cisneros is a first. He is the first American of Mexican descent ever elected mayor of an important U.S. city — San Antonio, Texas. Many people believe strongly that Henry Cisneros is one of the smartest and most promising politicians in America today.

When Henry Cisneros was the mayor, San Antonio was the tenth largest city in the United States. Despite modern constructions, San Antonio retains much of its Old World charm.

Mariachi bands play along *Paseo del Rio*, (River Walk), during the ten days of Fiesta San Antonio.

Henry is proud of his Mexican heritage. His grandfather, Jose Romulo Munguia y Torres, crossed the Rio Grande from Mexico into the United States in 1926. He settled in San Antonio, Texas. Like other immigrants before and after him, Munguia came seeking a better life for his family.

He worked hard, and, in time, bought a small house on the west side San Antonio.

In 1944, Munguia's daughter, Elvira, met George Cisneros, one of her brother's army buddies. Six months later, she and George were married. Two years later, on June 11, 1947, Henry Gabriel Cisneros was born.

Henry grew up in his grandfather's middle-class, Hispanic neighborhood. All the neighbors were good friends. They always helped each other. Many times they would come together and share holidays and other special occasions.

For four nights during Fiesta San Antonio, the La Villita Historical District (left) becomes a cultural fair. The *Escaramuza*, a precision sidesaddle riding team (above), made up of young women from 12 to 18, is part of the fiesta's *charreada*, or Mexican rodeo.

Henry's grandfather taught the family to be proud of their heritage. Sometimes the family would get together and study Mexican culture and history. Henry and his brothers and sisters — Pauline, George, Jr., Tina, and Tim — listened and learned.

Elvira and George Cisneros believed in hard work and education. They wanted their children to be successful. Mrs. Cisneros kept the children busy and out of trouble. Everyone had something special to do — even during summer vacation.

Henry's hobbies included building model airplanes and playing the piano. Sometimes he would write stories and poems with his brothers and sisters. He also liked to read. He liked it so much that one summer he read nearly fifty books!

Henry (first seat, row two) played French horn in his high school band. A leader in the sodality, Henry (standing top right, above) was interested in his own and his classmates spiritual development.

The family would talk for hours after dinner. George Cisneros and his children discussed different issues and current events.

Henry was smart and energetic. He was so smart that he was skipped from second to fourth grade.

The future mayor was challenged at Central Catholic High School. He studied and learned as much as he could. A teacher encouraged him to express himself by writing. When President John F. Kennedy was killed in 1963, Henry was sixteen. He wrote a poem about the president's death. It was selected as one of the most outstanding poems in all of San Antonio's high schools and was included in a special book of poetry.

Henry did well outside the classroom, too. He played the French horn and was executive officer in the ROTC. At this time he thought about having a military career like his father, who was a colonel, but college came first. After graduation from high school he entered Texas A & M University.

Soon, he became a class officer and was named outstanding cadet of his ROTC unit. Henry liked college. At first he had too much fun. A professor scolded him because some of his grades weren't good. Henry even had to repeat a course. It never happened again. Next time the young cadet received all A's! His new goal was to become the best and to "go for it!"

Thinking about the future, Henry decided he wanted a career in government. After graduation he began working for the cities of San Antonio and Bryan, Texas.

Later he worked for the Model Cities Program in San Antonio. This was an important government program that helped poor people. He enjoyed the work. Henry was very busy, but not too busy to marry his high-school sweetheart, Mary Alice Perez, on June 1, 1969.

Henry decided he didn't know enough about government even though he had a master's degree from Texas

Far left: Henry (in the first row, right) served on the student leadership committee in college at Texas A & M. *Left:* The year before he had been treasurer of the sophomore class, (Cisneros is second from left).

A & M University. So he and Mary Alice headed for Washington, D.C., where Henry enrolled at Georgetown University. He also began working at the National League of Cities.

At the League he learned about city problems and how to solve them. He also made a very important decision. He decided that someday he would return home and become mayor of San Antonio. He had a lot of work to do first, however. He must be prepared.

Washington, D.C., fascinated Henry. He decided to learn still more about government. He applied for a special program called the White House Fellows. If accepted, he would work in the White House or with one of the cabinet members. It was a great opportunity.

In 1971, Henry Cisneros became a White House Fellow. He was one of sixteen persons selected from a group

Mayor Cisneros conducts a bus tour of real estate sites available for development by private businesses.

Henry jogs with his daughter Teresa.

of three thousand! That same year his first daughter, Teresa, was born.

Henry's job was with Elliot Richardson, who was secretary of the Department of Health, Education, and Welfare. Again, Henry was able to work on city problems.

Elliot Richardson thought Henry was a talented and skillful young man. He liked him and encouraged Henry's political plans.

During Henry's last year as a White House Fellow he visited Africa and Asia. Returning to the United States, he decided to attend Harvard University in Cambridge, Massachusetts, for even more education. He later attended the Massachusetts Institute of Technology and was also a teacher. Henry received another master's degree and a doctorate, the highest college degree.

In August 1974, Henry and Mary Alice decided it was time to return home. Dr. Henry Cisneros would become an assistant professor at the University of Texas at San Antonio. The Cisneros family would eventually live in Grandfather Munguia's modest, gray frame house in the old west side neighborhood.

Everything was very confusing when Henry returned home. The Mexican Americans were struggling to gain political power. The whites who controlled city government were resisting them. Neither group trusted

Mary Alice and Henry Cisneros admire a neighbor's
child in their west side neighborhood.

the other. Hispanics had the voting
power — they were the largest single
ethnic group in the city. Now they
wanted to elect one of their own to
political office.

The search began for someone the
entire city could trust. People turned to
Henry Cisneros. Henry had the
government experience. A few people
thought he wasn't the right person for

the job. But after a while all agreed. The Hispanics backed Henry.

In 1975, Henry Cisneros became the youngest city councilman in San Antonio history. In that year his second daughter, Mercedes Christina, was born.

The new city councilman worked very hard to bring the people of San Antonio together. He always voted for the programs that he thought were best for the city. The people liked Henry.

The Cisneros family, from left to right: Mercedes, Henry, Teresa, Mary Alice

Before becoming mayor, Henry served on the city council (right) for six years.

They liked him so much they reelected him in 1977 and again in 1979.

A mayoral election was to be held in 1981. Henry thought about his political plans. This was really his big chance. He decided to run for mayor of San Antonio.

Family members, childhood friends, union leaders, young people, senior

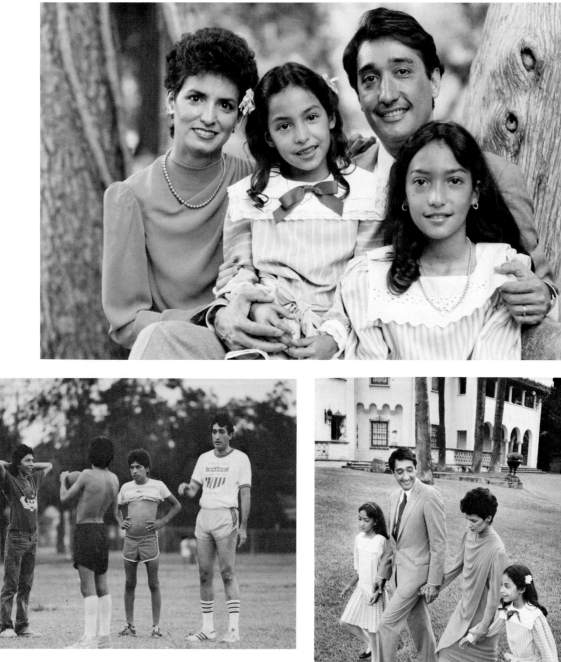

Devoted parents Henry and Mary Alice include Teresa and Mercedes in their public appearances. Wearing a T-shirt proclaiming San Antonio ''America's Town All-American 1983,'' Henry (above) plays football with the neighborhood boys.

citizens, political workers — everyone came together to work for Henry Cisneros.

They raised money, knocked on doors, talked on the telephone, gave speeches, and stuffed envelopes. It was a hard fight, but Henry Cisneros won! On April 4, 1981, he became the first Hispanic mayor of a major U.S. city. He took the oath of office on May 1.

The new mayor had to work harder than ever before. There were still some bad feelings after the election. So he continued working to bring everyone together.

Henry promised to get jobs for people and bring new high-tech business to the city. This was part of his economic growth program. San Antonio, like other cities in the United States, needed his help.

Mayor Cisneros studies telephone messages in his office.

In 1983, Henry was reelected by a very large vote. He had kept his promises. Things were improving in the city. People were getting along better, too.

By now, the entire country was talking about the young Mexican-American mayor from San Antonio. He was asked to give speeches and to talk to Congress and different groups all over the country.

In order to attract new businesses to the city, Mayor Cisneros traveled outside his state, gave speeches, and attended planning meetings with potential investors.

Mayor Cisneros takes Andrew Young, mayor of Atlanta, Georgia, along River Walk.

Reporters and writers from newspapers, magazines, and television and radio stations all wanted interviews with him. He had become a national figure. Henry was busier than ever. Even though he was mayor, he still kept his teaching job at the university.

The year 1984 proved to be very exciting for Mayor Cisneros. He was becoming more and more involved in national politics. Walter Mondale, who

Cisneros addresses the 1984 Democratic National Convention.

was running for president, was a friend. He asked Henry to speak at the Democratic National Convention and work with Hispanic delegates.

Not much later, Mondale interviewed Henry Cisneros in Minnesota. The presidential candidate almost chose Henry to be his vice-presidential running mate. Mondale finally picked Congresswoman Geraldine Ferraro instead.

In 1987, Henry ran for a fourth term as mayor. The people of San Antonio gave him a clear vote of confidence again. Henry's future looked very bright.

But on June 10, 1987—just one day before his fortieth birthday—his life changed. Henry and Mary Alice's third child and first son, John Paul Anthony, was born prematurely. The baby boy had a defective heart and would need constant care to survive his first year.

The problems with the new baby created more problems for Henry and Mary Alice. In 1988, San Antonio newspapers announced that the parents might get a divorce. With all the strain, Henry decided that four terms as San Antonio's mayor were enough. He left public office in 1988.

Over the next few years, Henry and Mary Alice overcame their problems. In the meantime, Henry concentrated on business. He earned good wages speaking in public on issues that concerned Texans. He also managed a group of businesses, including a small airplane service, from an office in San Antonio. Then he served briefly on the Federal Reserve Bank of Dallas. The Federal Reserve acts as central bankers for the U.S. government and some other banks.

By 1992, Henry Cisneros seemed interested in entering politics again. In May, he left his job at the Federal Reserve. He began working for the Texas campaign of presidential candidate Bill Clinton.

In November 1992, Bill Clinton won the presidential election. The president-elect must have remembered Henry's hard work. He quickly asked Henry to travel to Little Rock, Arkansas. There, a transition

Bill Clinton (right) and Al Gore (left) look on as new cabinet member
Henry Cisneros answers questions from the press.

team was searching for people to work for
the new president.

Many of the president's most
important workers join what is called the
cabinet. Members of the president's
cabinet have a great deal of responsibility.
Besides giving advice to the president,
they direct large departments of the
federal government.

In a matter of days, President-elect Clinton announced that he would like Henry to join his cabinet. If the U.S. Senate agreed, Henry Cisneros would become the Secretary of Housing and Urban Development (HUD). HUD has important responsibilities to improve living conditions in U.S. cities.

On January 12, 1993, Henry and fellow Texan and cabinet member Lloyd Bentsen met formally with U.S. senators. The senators agreed that both men would be excellent cabinet members.

Bill Clinton was inaugurated as president of the United States on January 20, 1993. The following day, January 21, a voice vote in the U.S. Senate made official the cabinet appointments of Henry Cisneros and fourteen other workers. For the new HUD secretary, the biggest and most exciting challenges are just beginning.

HENRY CISNEROS

1947   June 11 — Henry Gabriel Cisneros is born in San Antonio
1961   Attended Central Catholic High School
1964   Attended Texas A & M University
1969   June 1 — Married Mary Alice Perez
1970   Attended Georgetown University and worked for National League of Cities in Washington, D.C.
1971   Named White House Fellow; daughter Teresa is born
1973   Studied at Harvard University and Massachusetts Institute of Technology
1974   Returned to San Antonio and joined staff of University of Texas
1975   Elected to city council; daughter Mercedes is born
1976   Named one of the Five Outstanding Young Texans
1981   April 4 — elected mayor of San Antonio
1983   Reelected mayor; appointed to serve on Central American Commission
1984   Interviewed by Walter Mondale for vice-presidential position on Democratic ticket
1987   Reelected mayor for fourth term; son John Paul Anthony born
1988   Left office of mayor of San Antonio
1990   Manages own financial company
1993   Confirmed as Secretary of Housing and Urban Development (HUD)

INDEX

ABOUT THE AUTHOR

NAURICE ROBERTS has written numerous stories and poems for children. Her background includes work as a copywriter, television personality, commercial announcer, college instructor, communications consultant, and human resources trainer. She received a B.A. in Broadcast Communications from Columbia College in Chicago where she presently resides. Her hobbies include working with young people, lecturing, and jogging. She has written books about Andrew Young, Barbara Jordan, and Cesar Chavez.